NEW ZEALAND

NORTH AND SOUTH

First published in 2006 by Craig Potton Publishing
Reprinted 2007, 2008, 2009, 2010, 2011

Craig Potton Publishing
98 Vickerman Street, PO Box 555,
Nelson, New Zealand
www.craigpotton.co.nz

ISBN 10: 1-877333-58-1
ISBN 13: 978-1-877333-58-3

Printed in China by Everbest Printing Co. Ltd

CONTENTS

Left: Lake Gault, lying atop a glacial moraine in Westland/Tai Poutini National Park against the backdrop of the Southern Alps.
Above: Ohinemaka Beach, a wonderful sweep of South Westland coastline flanked by ancient dunes and wetlands.

Left: Morning mist lifts at Lake Mapourika, South Westland. *Above:* Juvenile nikau palms dominate this coastal forest in Paparoa National Park. *Overleaf:* Little Arch, Oparara Valley, Kahurangi National Park.

Above: Winter snow lies on the névés, ridges and summits of Westland/Tai Poutini National Park, seen in this aerial view taken at dusk. The broad névé to the right is the snowfield feeding the Franz Josef Glacier, while the prominent peak above the névé is Elie de Beaumont. *Right:* Three-thousand-metre peaks above Fox Glacier, from left, Mt Haast, Lendenfeld Peak, Mt Tasman and Torres Peak – each presenting considerable challenges to mountaineers.

Above: Franz Josef Glacier, Ka Roimata o Hine Hukatere, is one of the fastest moving glaciers in the world, averaging two to three metres a day. Since 1865, the glacier's terminal has retreated more than three kilometres and is continuing to retreat despite the occasional surge after a heavy winter.
Right: A dramatic aerial view of the Fox Glacier as it plunges to the lowlands from its tributary snowfields below Mt Tasman.

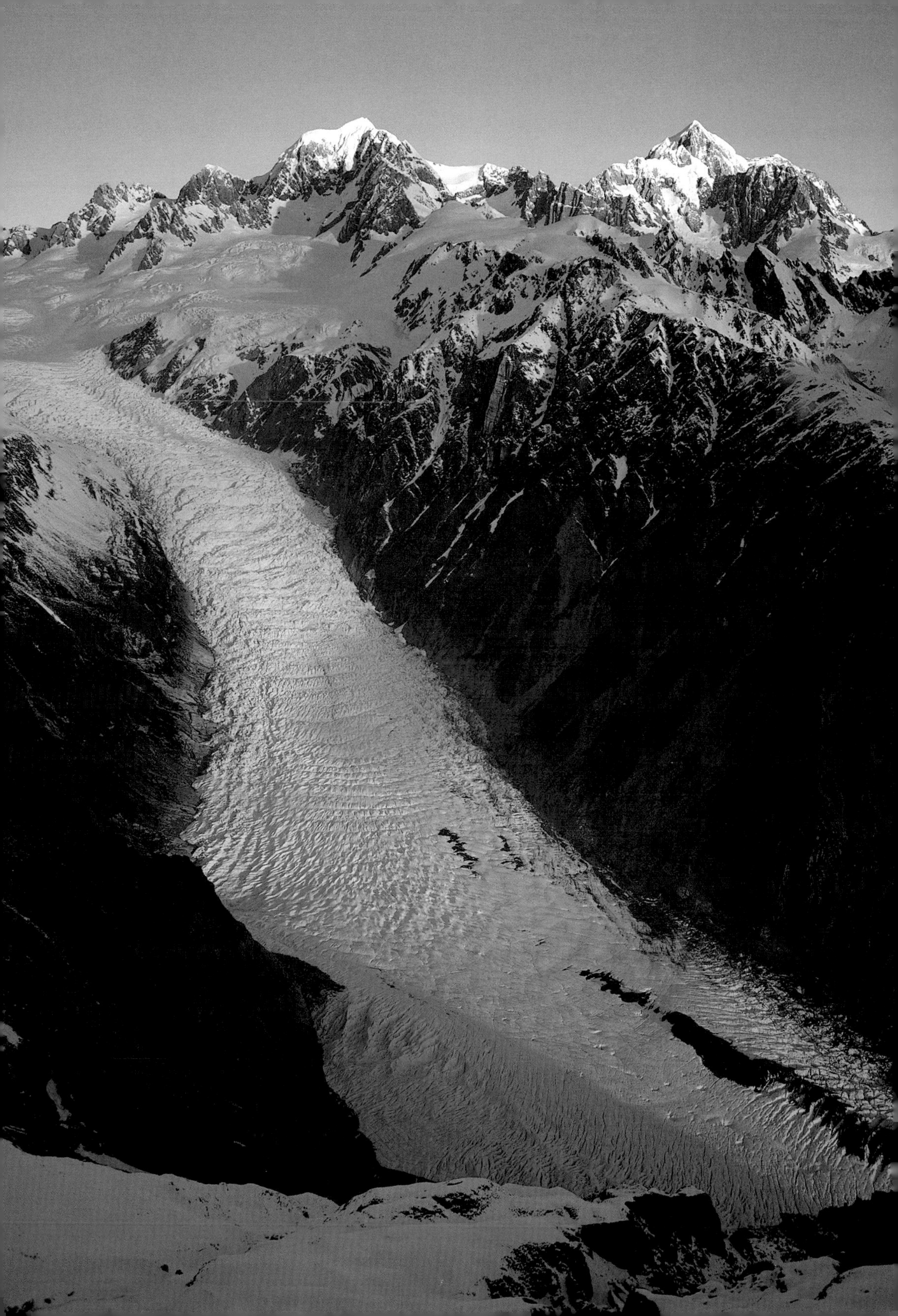

Left: The icy summits of Mt Tasman (pictured left) and Aoraki/Mt Cook rise dramatically above farmland near Fox Glacier village. At the base of the foothills is the boundary of two of the earth's continental plates – the Indo-Australasian and the Pacific. This fault – the Alpine Fault – is responsible for lifting the Southern Alps to their present height. *Above:* A remote homestead at Inangahua, in North Westland. *Overleaf:* Sunset at Lake Matheson near Fox Glacier.

Left: At Punakaiki in North Westland the wind, rain and sea have eroded spectacular canyons and blowholes from the limestone/mudstone rock, including the renowned pancake rocks at Dolomite Point. The blowholes are easily viewed from a walking track, and are most active when a southwesterly swell is running. *Above:* A walker dwarfed by the enormous overhang at the bottom of the Truman Track, a popular coastal track near Punakaiki. *Overleaf:* Lush South Westland rainforest.

Left: The south face of Aoraki/Mt Cook from the Hooker Valley, near the Hermitage.
Above: The Devil's Punchbowl, a short walk from Arthur's Pass village in Arthur's Pass National Park.
Previous page: Mt Tasman, with the Tasman Glacier beyond, Aoraki/Mount Cook National Park.

Above: The tussock-covered foothills on the eastern side of the Southern Alps are home to a string of vast high-country sheep stations. Here on a South Canterbury station a shepherd musters a flock of merino sheep, a breed favoured in this harsh country for their hardiness and for the lucrative ultra-fine wool they produce. *Right:* A country road near Lake Tekapo in the Mackenzie Country. *Previous page:* Fairlie pastureland under a thick blanket of snow.

Photograph: Andris Apse

Photograph: Andris Apse

Left: The Canterbury Plains reach west towards distant ranges and mountains. At 64 kilometres wide, and almost 200 kilometres long, the plains are the largest expanse of flat land in New Zealand. *Above:* A spring arrival on a New Zealand farm.

Left: Cathedral Square, Christchurch. The Gothic architecture of the nineteenth-century Cathedral contrasts with the work of twenty-first century sculptor, Neil Dawson, whose 18-metre-high *Chalice* was erected to celebrate the new millennium and the 150th anniversary of the founding of the city. *Above:* A tram route links Cathedral Square with the latest architectural statement, the new Christchurch Art Gallery, Te Puna o Waiwhetu, which opened in 2003. *Overleaf:* The ice ramparts of Aoraki/Mt Cook, New Zealand's highest peak at 3754 metres, in Aoraki/Mount Cook National Park.

Far left: The half-day walk from the Milford Road to Key Summit is rewarded with fine views from a forest-fringed alpine wetland toward Mt Christina in Fiordland's Darran Mountains. *Left:* Lake Te Anau is one of Fiordland National Park's large and beautiful glacier-formed lakes. *Above:* Stunning glaciated peaks above Milford Sound.

Left: Queenstown, picturesquely sited on the shores of Lake Wakatipu beneath The Remarkables, is often dubbed the country's adventure capital. *Above:* Bungy jumping, jetboating, rafting, skiing, paragliding, mountainbiking and mountaineering are among the adventurous activities to be enjoyed here. *Previous page:* Lake Hawea, a narrow glacial lake, is the smallest of the southern alpine lakes.

Above: The clear pools of the Clinton River at Clinton Forks on the southern leg of Fiordland's Milford Track. *Right*: Morning mist clears from Campbell's Kingdom near Doubtful Sound in Fiordland National Park.

Left: The intriguing Moeraki Boulders on Moeraki Beach, Otago, are 60 million years old. *Above:* Colonies of yellow-eyed penguins breed on the Otago Peninsula.

Far left: Sutherland Falls, the fifth highest waterfall in the world, drains Lake Quill and plunges into the Arthur Valley, on the Milford Track. *Above:* Red and silver beech forest in Fiordland's Eglinton valley. *Left:* Fiordland was the last place on the mainland where native kakapo, a flightless parrot, were found. Under severe threat of extinction from introduced predators, the last kakapo were removed and placed on offshore islands. Fewer than 100 birds remain today.
Overleaf: A sparkling winter's morning at Milford Sound after a southerly clearance, in Fiordland National Park.

Photograph: Dennis Buurman

Left: Once hunted to near extinction, sperm whales are now the focus of a major whale-watching industry at Kaikoura, south of Blenheim.
Above: New Zealand fur seals, which breed along the Kaikoura coast, and dolphins (common dolphin at left, dusky dolphin at right) are common sights, much to the delight of visitors.
Overleaf: Abel Tasman National Park.

Above: The sheltered bays and coves of the Marlborough Sounds, ancient valleys drowned by rising seas, are a modern-day yachting paradise. Yachts are seen here moored near Lochmara Bay, in Queen Charlotte Sound.
Right: In this aerial view are the forested ridges of Mt Richmond Forest Park, Pelorus Sound, Admiralty Bay and D'Urville Island on the edge of Cook Strait.

Left: Nelson Haven, the Boulder Bank and Tasman Bay, from Nelson's Port Hills looking towards the Abel Tasman Coast. Nelson City (population 43,500) is a thriving regional centre, a hub for the tourism, horticulture, forestry and fishing industries, and increasingly a place for wealthy retirees. *Above:* Vast areas of the Wairau valley have been converted to vineyards – Marlborough is now the country's largest wine region, and is world famous for the quality of its Sauvignon Blanc.

Far left: Awaroa Inlet, Abel Tasman National Park.
Left: Tree ferns line a streamway near the coast.
Above: Sea kayaking is a popular Abel Tasman coast experience, providing opportunities to encounter seals, dolphins, penguins and other coastal wildlife. Kayakers also see the park's impressive granite headlands and secluded sandy bays.

Above: Abel Tasman National Park's sublime forest-fringed bays and golden-sand beaches are connected by the most popular tramping route in New Zealand – the Coast Track. At Pukatea Bay, a tramper takes a break to stroll along the edge of this perfect crescent beach. At high summer, the park's beaches are packed with people who have arrived on foot, or by yacht, boat or kayak. *Right:* Torrent Bay.

Left: Waitemata Harbour and Auckland's central city skyline. *Above:* In a city mad about yachting, it's no surprise that one in ten Aucklanders owns a boat or yacht, many of which are moored in Westhaven Marina.

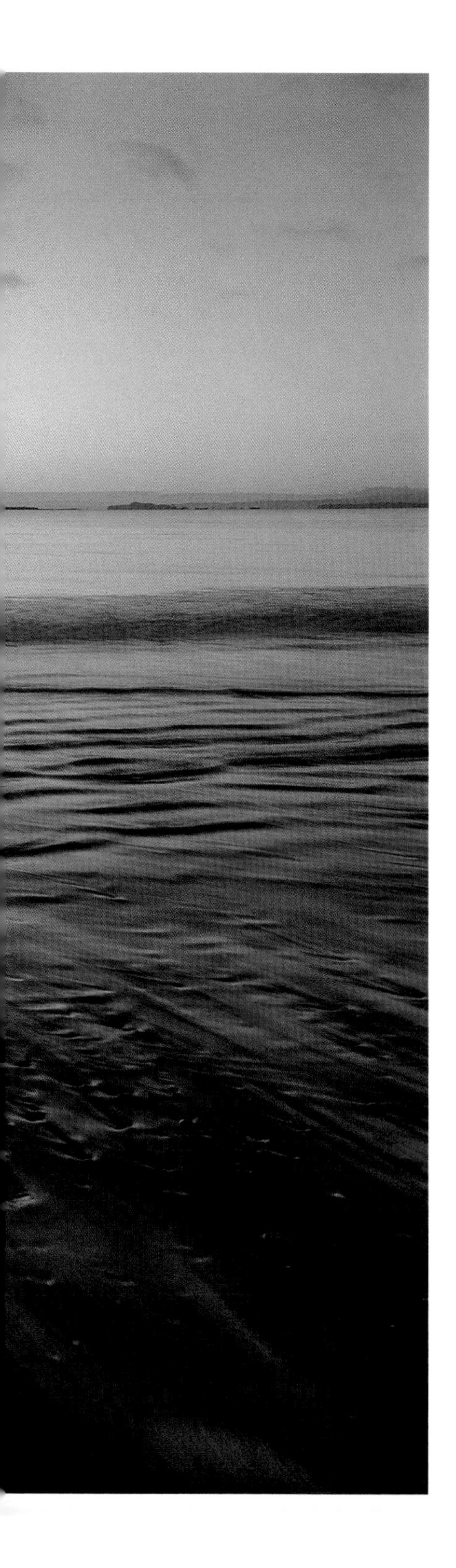

Left: Rangitoto Island in the Hauraki Gulf last erupted just 600 years ago. A visit to the island, a protected reserve, is a popular day excursion from Auckland. *Top:* Pohutukawa blooms on Little Barrier Island, one of the most important of New Zealand's island sanctuaries for native species. *Above:* A rock stack at sunset on Whatipu Beach at the entrance to Auckland's Manukau Harbour.

Left: Tane Mahuta, the largest kauri in New Zealand, in Waipoua Forest, Northland. *Above:* Cathedral Cove and the adjacent marine reserve are a short walk from Hahei on the Coromandel Peninsula.

Far left: Among the Far North's treasures are the expansive dunelands of Te Paki Farm Park at the top of Ninety Mile Beach. The farm park is a scattered series of reserves providing habitat for native flora and fauna. *Left:* A few kilometres on, Cape Reinga is the place where Maori believe the spirits depart after death to be borne by ocean currents to their mythical home in Hawaiiki. *Above:* Bay of Islands.

Above: The Whanganui River is New Zealand's longest navigable river, used from the earliest days of human occupation as an access route from the coast to the Central North Island hinterland. Its upper reaches flow through Whanganui National Park. Canoeing down the river is the park's most popular recreational activity.

Top: The beautiful limestone caves of the Waitomo area lie west of the Central North Island's volcanic heartland. Thousands of visitors a year enter this accessible cave system with its spectacular caverns, underground waterways, glowworm grottos and extraordinary formations of stalactites.
Above: Whanganui National Park's virgin and regenerating forest contains populations of North Island brown kiwi. *Previous page:* The June 1996 eruption of Mt Ruapehu, in Tongariro National Park.

Far left: Pohutu Geyser, one of Rotorua's world-renowned geothermal wonders. *Above:* The sparkling waters and mineral deposits in Waiotapu's Champagne Pool. The pool was formed 900 years ago by a hydrothermal explosion. *Left:* Geothermal mudpools near Rotorua are thicker in summer when there is less rainwater. *Previous pages:* Snow-streaked Mt Ngauruhoe (foreground) and Mt Ruapehu at sunrise, Tongariro National Park.

Left and above: Mt Taranaki (2518 m), in Egmont National Park, is the most recent in a chain of volcanoes that have stood in the area north of the present peak over the past two million years. Mt Taranaki attracts climbers and trampers all year round. *Top:* Bells Falls is one of the highlights of the popular Around-the-Mountain Circuit.

Top: This tranquil image of Lake Taupo belies the lake's devastating origins: a huge volcanic eruption – one of the largest ever in the world – thought to have occurred about 2000 years ago. The lake was stocked with trout in the nineteenth century and is now a renowned fly fishing destination. *Right:* The mountains of Tongariro National Park are sacred to the Ngati Tuwharetoa tribe whose wharenui/meeting house is located at Waihi on the shores of Lake Taupo. *Above:* Just north of Taupo, the 425-kilometre Waikato River is channelled through a narrow gut before it crashes spectacularly over the 11-metre Huka Falls.

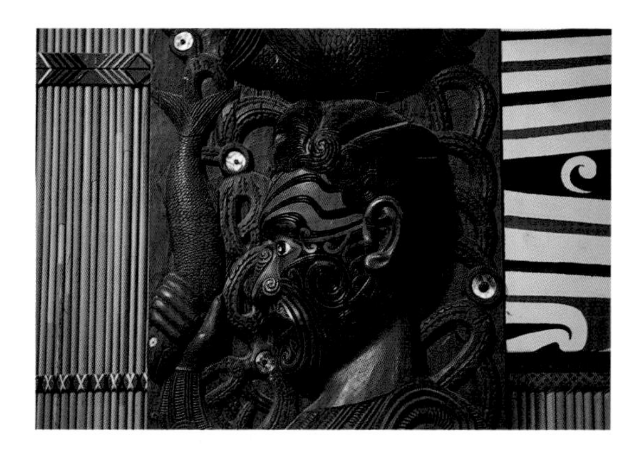

Left: The North Island's east coast is a spectacular combination of bluffs, headlands and beaches. The bluffs of Cape Kidnappers jut into the Pacific at the southern end of Hawke Bay. New Zealand's largest colony of Australasian gannets nests on the Cape. *Top:* The blend of Maori and European culture in Hawkes Bay and the East Cape is often exemplified in its art and architecture: the National Tobacco Company building is one of Napier's most famous art deco structures. *Above:* The Ruatoria Memorial Hall contains intricate Maori carvings and panels. *Previous pages:* Pohutukawa flowering at Wainui Beach, near Gisborne.

Left and above: Rolling hill-country in the Tukituki valley, south of Havelock North, is prime sheep-farming country, Hawkes Bay's most important industry. The region's drier climate has also been a boon for farm forestry, winemaking and market gardening.
Previous page: Korokoro Falls near Lake Waikaremoana in Te Urewera National Park

Above: Te Papa Tongarewa, or 'Te Papa' is New Zealand's national museum. Opened in 1998, it quickly became a domestic and international tourist drawcard. Te Papa houses important national collections of Maori, Pacific and European art and culture and tells the stories of New Zealand's unique flora and fauna and the dynamic forces that shaped the land, and of its discovery by Pacific voyagers and later European colonisers.

Above: The Cable Car (which links Wellington City with Victoria University and the Botanic Gardens) is another icon in a city also renowned for its nightlife and cafés.
Previous page: Dawn, Oriental Bay, Wellington.

Photograph: Kevin Judd

Left: Martinborough's vineyards produce some of the nation's finest wines. *Above:* Castlepoint, on the Wairarapa coast.